Chrissy CUPCAKE

6 - 12 YEARS

Shows you how to make healthy energy giving cupcakes

STEP BY STEP INSTRUCTION
in cupcake making & other interesting food information

Children love to learn new things, why not be their teacher and go on the journey of learning how to cook together...?

If you have purchased this book without its cover, it may be a stolen book.
Neither the publisher or the author is under any obligation to provide professional services in anyway, legal, health or in any form which is related to this book, its contents advice or otherwise.

The law and practices vary from country to country and state to state. If legal or professional information is required, the purchaser, or the reader should seek the information privately and best suited to their particular needs, and circumstances.
The author and publisher specifically disclaim any liability that may be incurred from the information within this book.
All rights reserved.
No part of this book, including the interior design, images, cover design, diagrams, or any intellectual property (IP), icons and photographs may be reproduced or transmitted in any form by any means (electronic, photocopying, recording or otherwise) without the prior permission of the publisher. ©

Copyright© 2020 MSI Australia
All rights reserved.

ISBN: 978-0-6481884-9-0

Published by Books For Reading On Line.com
Under licence from MSI Ltd, Australia
Company Registration No: 642923859
NSW, Australia
See our website: www.booksforreadingonline.com
Or contact by email: admin@booksforreadingonline.com
Covers and Copyright owned by MSI, Australia

MSI acknowledges the author and images used in this book.

www.how2books.com.au
booksforreadingonline.com

Contents   Page

Learning how to cook	1
Using honey instead of sugar – it's so much healthier	2
Cooking tools you will need to know about	3
Dangers in the kitchen	7
Cooking tips	8
Why is it so important to know about the food you eat?	9
Understanding organic food	14
You will need these ingredients to make honey and yogurt cupcakes	18
Basic honey and yogurt cupcakes	19
You will need these ingredients to make butter, honey rosette, cream	21
Butter, honey, and rosette cream topping	22
Cream topped basic cupcakes	23
You will need these ingredients to make lemon-zest cupcakes	24
Lemon-zest cupcakes with lemon topping	25
You will need these ingredients to make orange and mandarin-zest cupcakes	27
Orange and mandarin-zest cupcakes	28
You will need these ingredients to make these mango jelly cupcakes	30
Mango jelly cupcakes	31
You will need these ingredients to make these raspberry jelly cupcakes	33
Raspberry jelly cupcakes	34
You will need these ingredients to make these chocolate cupcakes	37
Chocolate cupcakes	38
Honey and sugar-free blueberry cupcakes	40
You will need these ingredients to make these honey and sugar-free blueberry cupcakes	41
Honey and sugar-free blueberry cupcakes	42
Little treats for special people	44
You will need these ingredients to make these cheese and honey cupcakes	45
Cheese and honey cupcakes	46
Chrissy cupcake says	49

Learning how to cook

Chrissy Cupcake says,

'Learning about the food you eat is great fun. Eating good food helps to keep you healthy. When you eat junk food, you can feel sick and awful.

Healthy food allows you to play, have fun, learn your lessons when you are at school, and allows you to help mum and dad if they need a hand.

Natural, healthy food is grown in good, healthy soil. When vegetables and fruit grow in healthy soil, they pass on their goodness to you as you eat and enjoy your food. Animals that live on the land and when they also eat healthy grass and natural herbs that grow on the land, they too, pass on their goodness in the form of the meat you eat. When our oceans are clean, we catch the healthy fish, crabs and prawns who live in the oceans; these foods are good for your health, body, brain, and mind.

If the soil and the oceans are not healthy, our food will not be healthy and is not good to eat.

Cupcakes made from healthy ingredients are fun to make and eat. They are fun at birthday parties and for special times. Not all cupcakes have to be sweet, some can be made from savoury produce like herbs and different cheeses.

Before you start to cook, there are some things you need to know.

First, you need to think, how do you feel, are you in the mood to do some cooking today? The food you eat needs to be made with love, so if you are not in the mood to cook, please do not cook. When you cook your food, it should be done with love and care. When this is done, your food will not only taste better, but you will also love the learning you do.

Learning how to cook is for both boys and girls.'

Using honey instead of sugar – is so much healthier...

Cooking tools you will need and need to know about

Cupcakes can be made in different sizes. You can make small or larger cupcakes. For the quantities of ingredients used in the recipes in this book you can make 6 large cupcakes or 12 smaller cupcakes.

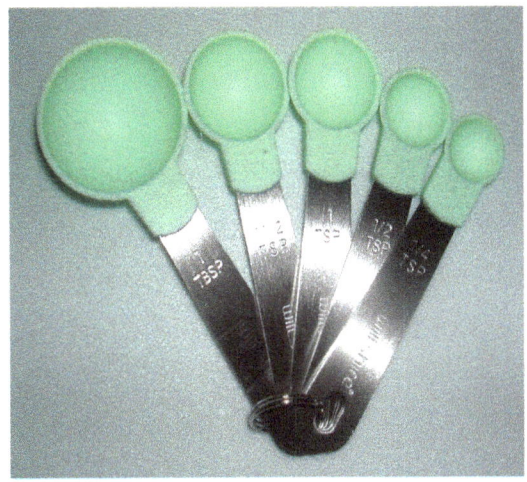

Measuring spoons for measuring small amounts.

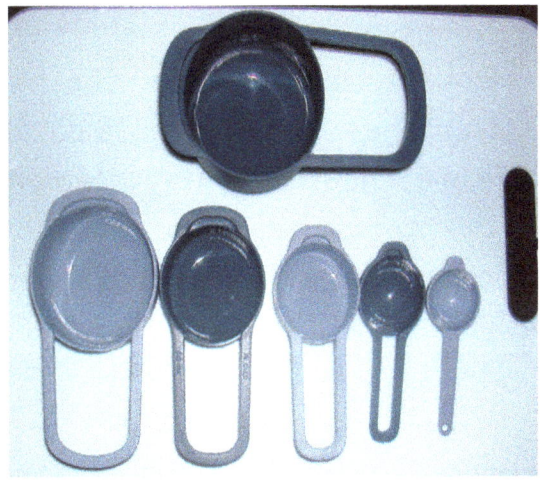

Measuring spoons for measuring larger amounts.

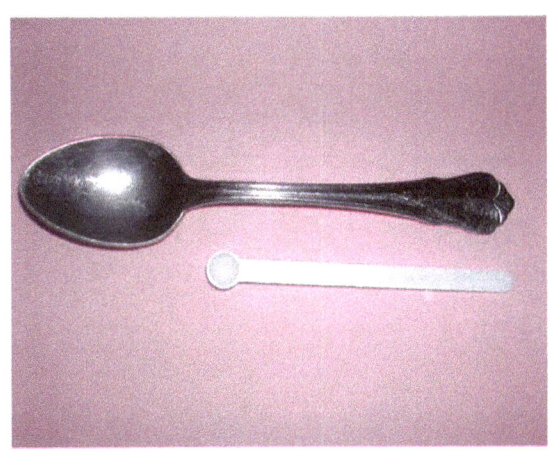

If you use Pure Stevia as a sweetener in your cupcakes, because of the intense sweetness, use only the white smaller spoon size, as indicated in the above picture, for measuring.

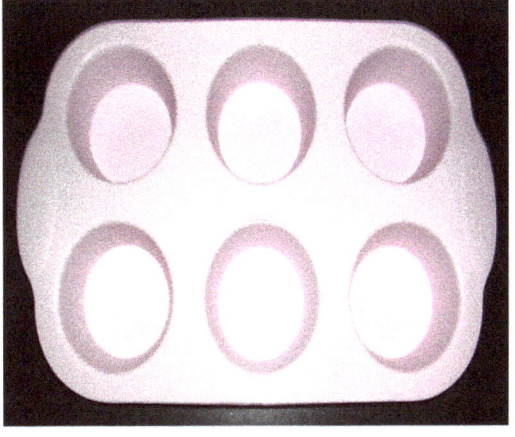

These cupcake cases are made from silicone and are 6 larger cupcake sizes, they can also bend when full of cupcake mix. You will need to put a baking tray under the silicone cupcake holder before putting your mixture into the cups and putting them into the oven.

Here you can see smaller cupcake cases, these are also, made out of silicone, and need to be placed on a baking tray before you fill the cupcake cases with your cupcake mix.

Some cupcake tins are made from metal. Above, you can see there are 12 cases; these will make a smaller cupcake.

Above, you can see a 6 case, tin. This can be used for baking muffins or large cupcakes.

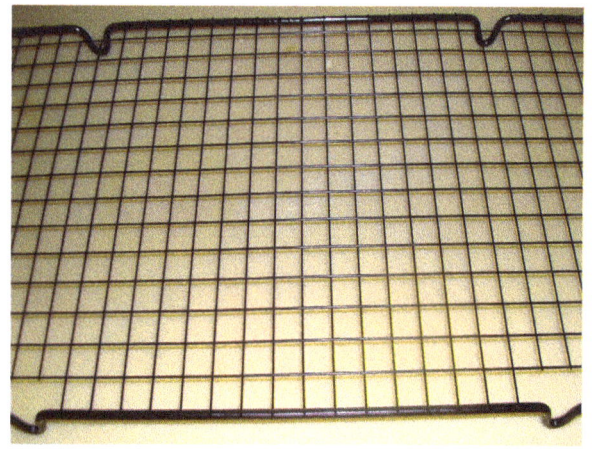
Cooling rack for your cupcakes and other cakes.

These are paper unbleached cupcake case used in a tin, cupcake cooking tray.

Lightweight cutting boards can be easier to work with small amounts of food. If you want to cut fruit like raspberries, blueberries and strawberries, a light weight cutting board is a good choice.

There are different weights in cutting boards. You will need a heavier weight to cut vegetables, fruit, or butter.

Large mixing bowl in plastic, ceramic, or glass.

A plastic citrus squeezer allows you to squeeze different citrus fruits and to collect their tasty juice that can be used in your recipes.

Different kitchen tools that you can collect over time. Here you can see:

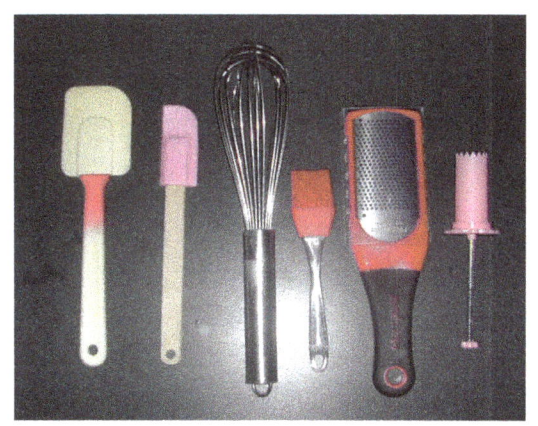

A stick blender can be used to blitz many fruit and vegetables.
Please see page 7: Dangers in the kitchen.

1) 2 spatulas for removing the last tasty cupcake mix from the bowl,
2) a whisk for whisking eggs or cream,
3) a pastry brush when you need to oil a cupcake tin or brush a cake, pastry or pie with egg or milk,
4) a zest grater for zesting the peel of oranges, lemons, limes, apples and other fruit or vegetables that need to be zested or grated, and
5) a plastic cutting tool for cutting the centre out of some cupcakes tops if you slice the top off the cupcake or for making cut circles in

Dangers in the kitchen

Please note: Chrissy Cupcake says: *'All children **must** be supervised when using electrical or cooking implements such as electric or battery operated beaters, stirring food in a saucepan on the lighted or heated stove or putting food into or taking from a heated oven.*

Also, the use of sharp knives and any cutting tools need to be explained to the child or children.

When walking with a knife, it must always be carried with its blade pointing towards to floor and should never be raised or pointed at another person.

When working with a gas or electric cooker, children need to understand the differences between gas and electric cooking. When a gas stove is turned on and there is not a flame an adult must be told. Children need to learn the difference of lighted gas and unlit gas.

The use of electrical tools also needs to be spoken about. Children need to understand that electrical appliances and water do not mix.'

Cooking tips

1) Always wash your hands before you start to cook or collect your cooking utensils, including your food ingredients.
2) Do not cook if you are not feeling well.
3) If the floor becomes wet, make sure you immediately wipe the moisture from the floor.
4) Make sure you keep your working area clean and tidy as you work.
5) Once you have decided what to cook, make sure everything is on the bench and easy to reach.
6) Warm the oven and oil the baking tray cups you are going to use.
7) Take your time, do not hurry when you are cooking, that is when accidents happen.
8) Understand the learning you are doing and discover that preparing your food is a pleasure.
9) When you have finished, do not walk away, and leave a mess for somebody else to clean up.
10) Wait patiently for your food to cook; do not open the oven door too soon, you may make your cupcakes go flat.
11) Talk to your family about the food you eat and ask them for their opinion when you have made something.
12) You will make mistakes, that is part of learning, but never, never give up, try, and try again. Every time you try, you learn something new.
13) Think about your food and don't be afraid to learn to taste something new.

Why is it so important to understand about the food you eat?

Chrissy Cupcake says:

'...Preparing children to take responsibility for the food they eat is part of growing up. When children learn about the quality of their food and how the food, they eat, reflects on how they feel and play, children become interested in the role food plays in their lives. When they have eaten something that makes them feel sick, they try not to eat that same food again. Some foods can taste good, but they may not be good to eat because it makes a child sick. Such food includes many take away food and drink meals bought at fast food chains, fast food outlets and other food convenience stores.

Molecules

'Food is made up of molecules. There are 4 food molecules. These molecules are: Fats, Protein, Carbohydrates and Alcohol.

Some molecules are made up of nasty food molecules in the form of food additives, while other food contain good food molecules which naturally develop in our food. Food molecules come in a similar shape but may vary in size. They resemble the shape of a triangle and are three-dimensional.

Good Food Molecule

Nasty Food Molecule

Hold your hand in front of you and bend your index finger to form a triangle shape and there you will see a similar shape to a molecule. Molecules can be small, smaller than a pin prick, but once you eat your food, your body's system recognises both the good and nasty food molecules.

Many commercially bought children and adult foods now contain nasty molecules. To teach children about eating a healthy diet can be fun for you, your family and friends. On a daily basis, we all need to eat, good, healthy food containing healthy molecules. Good molecules in our food not only keep our body, brain and mind healthy, they help us to enjoy life. Good molecules give good food energy. Nasty molecules can reduce energy, build up in our bodies and make us sick.

'Nasty food molecules can interfere with playtime and fun time. Children may feel tired because the food they have eaten is not right for their body and our body responds by making us feel sick and unwell. Nasty food molecules can also stay in our body and build up over a lifetime. Nasty molecules are usually put into fizzy drinks, junk food, many lollies and sweets, iced buns, doughnuts, and cakes, some

chocolate bars, health bars and other food bought at the supermarket, convenience stores or take away outlets. Of course, not all food bought has nasty molecules but some do. When you and your child or children are out shopping, please take some time to read the food ingredients panel on the side of the food box or wrapper.

Additive numbers

'Unhealthy molecules usually come in food additive numbers. Food additive numbers help to keep the food longer, change the colour of the food so that it looks good to eat, make it taste better than it really does and to appeal to our taste buds because the last time we ate something nice, we want to repeat that same experience again!

'As you and your children learn about the food you eat, you will become aware of how different food can make you feel well, help your body to stay healthy and your brain and mind work. When you eat healthy food, the task that was once difficult to do, or learning something new will become easier and a fun time.

Understanding the food in the recipes

'As you work through the recipes, Chrissy Cupcake will work with you to explain how the different ingredients help the food to be good food to make and eat. First, you need to know the difference between good and not so good food.'

Understanding organic food

Chrissy Cupcake speaks about organic and non-organic food...

'Organic means, foods that are from the natural environment. It also means there are no form of additives, fertiliser, growth hormones, growth regulators, pesticides, herbicides, or synthetic chemicals used in the growing production, or production of the produce. The word Organic also identifies that the plant or plant materials are not genetically modified (GMO) or contain modified organisms.

Organic Butter – is made from cows that are free to eat in healthy pastures. They are happy and enjoy the natural green pasture, sunshine, and showers of rain. They don't eat from pastures that have fertilisers, pesticides, herbicides or any synthetic chemicals added to the pasture, therefore, their milk makes very good butter. Most butters, even organic, can contain some trans fat. Natural, small quantities of trans fat can come from plants and grass. However, some butters may have synthetic trans fat that does not come from the natural grass the cows have eaten.

Non-Organic Butter – many margarines are sold as tasting like butter or as good as butter. Margarine is made in a different process to organic butter. Many margarines have a range of different additives to make it look and taste like butter, but it is not butter. By reading the ingredient panel on the side of the tub, you will be able to see the added additives.

Organic Honey – comes from healthy bees that have buzzed around and collected natural pollen from naturally growing plants. Natural honey has a sweet honey scent, it contains pollen collected by bees, wax and propolis[1].

Factory Made Honey – is not a natural food and is not made by bees but is made in a factory. It either has no smell or can smell sour; it contains no pollen, wax or propolis; it contains sugar cane, beet, or corn sugars all of which can be poisonous to your body. It does not crystalize as honey does and is not healthy to eat.

Organic Flour – is harvested from grains grown in healthy soil that do not have of additives, fertiliser, growth hormones, growth regulators, pesticides, herbicides, or synthetic chemicals used in the growing production, or production of the flour.

Non-Organic Flour - Many flours bought at the supermarket and other food stores are not organic. They may have many chemicals and food additives added, some of these chemicals include the additive food numbers:

    150d Caramel IV
    173 Aluminium
    220 Sulphur dioxide

---

[1] Propolis is a type of resin that is naturally made by bees and is collected from flower buds, flowers, grasses and cone bearing trees.

223 Sodium metabisulphite
281 Sodium propionet
342 Ammonium phosphates (i) Ammonium dihydrogen phosphate (ii) Diammonium hydrogen phosphate.

These are long words to remember but if you remember the numbers, it is not as difficult. Chrissy Cupcake also says, there are many more additives in some bought flours.

Natural Organic Yogurt – is good to eat from the tub but it is also good to cook with. Natural organic yogurt does not have any sugar added, you can always add natural organic honey to yogurt, and it tastes good. Also adding freshly chopped fruit makes a good snack after school. Yogurt is also good for young growing bones, teeth, nails, and hair.

Sugar Added Yogurt – many yogurts in small child-sized tubs say, they are a good child's snack but when you read the ingredient side panel, you can see the number of different additives used. Some of these are not good for children and contain many spoons of sugar that help to destroy teeth, store in the body and can help to create bad eating habits.

Organic Eggs – if you have hens and can collect your eggs from your chickens daily, you know you are eating good eggs. Eggs are very good for your eyesight, growing bones and are high in protein. Protein gives you energy to do things you want to do each day.

Natural organic gelatin – natural gelatin comes from animals such as beef who have lived a happy life in the fields where natural pasture grows and the farmer has not used any fertilisers, chemicals or pesticides. When looking to buy gelatin, buy unflavoured 225 bloom, this is a high-grade product. High grade gelatin is a protein, and our body does not make protein, it needs to come from the food we eat. Protein is essential for good health and wellbeing of every person on the planet. By eating gelatin, you provide your body with the protein it needs. Protein contains amino acids. Gelatin, in the form of protein, provides 8 of the 9 amino acids that are essential for good health.

With gelatin providing the protein, it helps you to digest your food, build up your bones and teeth and helps you to create a healthy immune system which helps to keep you healthy.

You will need these ingredients to make honey and yogurt cupcakes

80g softened organic butter

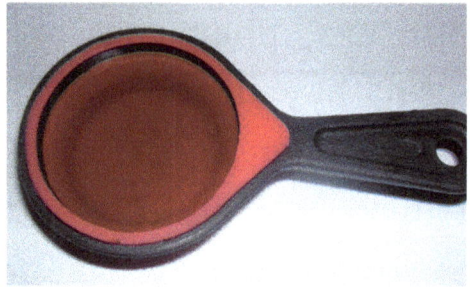

1/3 cup organic honey

1 organic egg

1 cup organic self raising flour

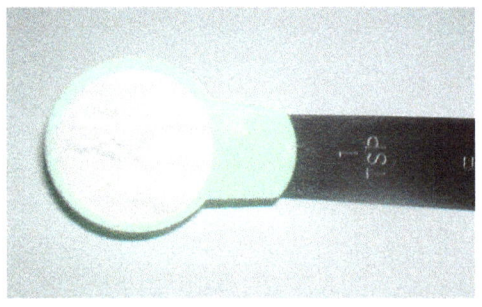

½ Tsp organic, non-aluminium baking powder

1 Tsp pure vanilla extract

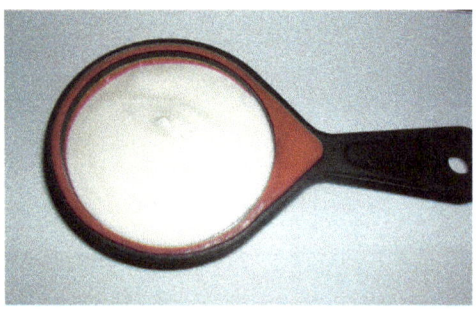

½ cup organic yogurt or milk

Cupcakes
Basic honey and yogurt cupcakes

Ingredients

80g organic softened salted butter
1/3 cup organic honey
1 large organic egg
1 cup organic self raising flour
½ Tsp organic, non-aluminium baking powder
1 Tsp pure vanilla extract
½ cup organic yogurt.

Preparation Time

15 minutes.

Cooking Time

40 minutes or until golden brown.

Oven temperature

Heat oven to 160° before putting the cupcakes into the oven to cook.

Tips

Chrissy Cupcake uses pre-cut paper cupcake cases to avoid using printed or inked cases. If you are thinking of having cupcakes for a child's party, why not create a case that is different and pretty.

Cupcake Method

- Beat butter and honey until creamed (if you have an electric beater it's far easier to use than doing this by hand)
- Add egg and beat into butter and honey mixture
- Add the vanilla extract
- When the butter, honey, egg, and vanilla are creamed, slowly add the flour, milk, and baking powder
- To keep the mixture light, it is crucial to add the flour slowly
- Beat until the mixture looks a light cream in colour
- Spoon into the cupcake cases and bake.

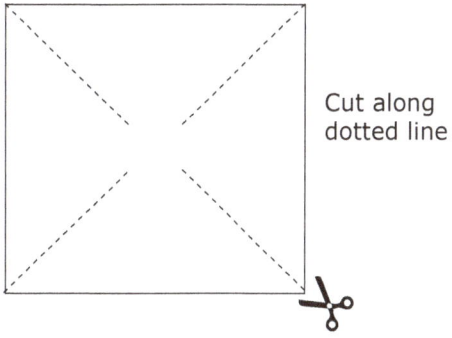

Cut along dotted line

Cut brown, unbleached paper into the required size to fit the shape of the cupcake case in the pan you are using.

Mixing butter, honey, and egg together.

The cupcake mix is spooned into the homemade cupcake cases ready for baking.

Golden cupcakes ready to eat or decorate.

With some fresh fruit for garnishing, basic cupcakes can be made to look delightful and fun to eat.

You will need these ingredients to make butter, honey, rosette, cream

60g softened organic butter

1 dstspn organic honey

1 organic egg yolk

2 dstspn organic arrowroot

1 – 2 dstspn organic milk

1 dstspn organic honey

Butter, honey, and rosette cream topping

Ingredients

Butter cream topping

60g salted, softened organic butter
1 organic egg yolk
1 dstspn organic honey
1 Tsp pure vanilla extract
2 dstspn organic arrowroot
1-2 dstspn organic milk if required.

Preparation Time

15 minutes.

Tips

This creamy, buttery topping can be used to fill and top a range of dessert cakes – a handy resource when you want to avoid commercially made cream or dessert decoration products.

When buying arrowroot, check the ingredient panel at the side of the product. Many commercially made products have sulphur dioxide (220) added as part of the ingredient. This should be **Avoided**.

Method

- Beat butter and honey until creamed (if you have an electric beater it will make a smooth paste)
- Once the butter and honey are creamed, add the vanilla and egg yolk to the butter mixture
- Slowly add the arrowroot
- Cream all ingredients together
- Spoon a small amount onto each cupcake
- With the back of a fork, swirl to form a rosette shape.

Butter cream topping spooned on to the top of each cupcake.

Cream topped basic cupcakes...

Pretty butter and honey cream rosette cupcakes ready to serve.

You will need these ingredients to make lemon-zest cupcakes

80g softened organic butter

1/3 cup organic honey

1 organic egg

1 cup organic self raising flour

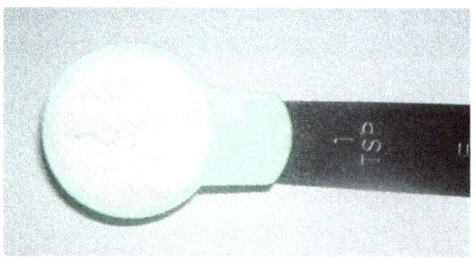
½ Tsp organic, non-aluminium baking powder

1 Tsp pure vanilla extract

½ cup organic yogurt or milk

Juice of ½ freshly squeezed organic lemon

Lemon-zest cupcakes with lemon butter topping

Please use either organic milk or yogurt in the following recipe.

Ingredients

80g organic softened salted butter
1/3 cup organic honey
1 large organic egg
1 cup organic self raising flour
½ Tsp organic, non-aluminium baking powder
1 Tsp pure vanilla extract
½ cup organic yogurt or milk
Juice ½ squeezed organic lemon
Zest of lemon peel.

Preparation Time

15 minutes.

Cooking Time

40 minutes or until golden brown.

Oven temperature

Heat oven to 160° before putting the cupcakes into the oven to cook.

Lemon zest topping

Butter cream topping

60g salted, softened organic butter
1 organic egg yolk
1 dstspn organic honey
1 Tsp pure vanilla extract
2 dstspn organic arrowroot
1-2 dstspn organic milk if required
1 Tsp freshly squeezed organic lemon juice.

Cupcake Method

- Beat butter and honey until creamed (if you have an electric beater it's far easier to use than doing this by hand)
- Add egg and beat into butter and honey mixture
- Add the vanilla extract
- Add the juice of the lemon
- When the butter, honey, egg, lemon and vanilla are creamed, slowly add the flour, milk and baking powder
- To keep the mixture light, it is crucial to add the flour slowly
- Beat until the mixture looks a light cream in colour
- Spoon into the cupcake cases and bake.

Lemon zest topping

- Beat butter and honey until creamed
- Once the butter and honey are creamed, add the vanilla, and egg yolk to the butter mixture
- Slowly add the arrowroot and lemon juice
- Cream all ingredients together
- When cool, top your cupcakes with this delicious butter cream and lemon icing.

Tip

You can add extra zest to your cupcake mixture by adding a little grated lemon peel.

Please ask a parent or adult to help you grate the peel.

The freshly beaten ingredients are in their cases waiting to be baked.

Baked, golden-brown cupcakes are allowed to cool before adding the zesty-lemon topping.

You will need these ingredients to make orange and mandarin-zest cupcakes

80g softened organic butter

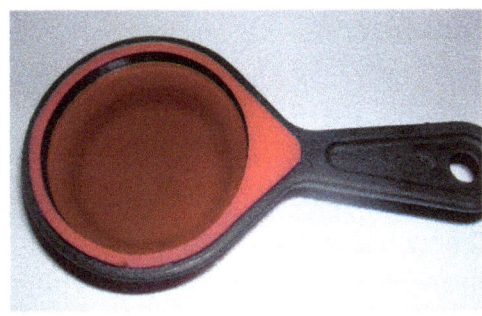
1/3 cup organic honey

1 organic egg

1 cup organic self raising flour

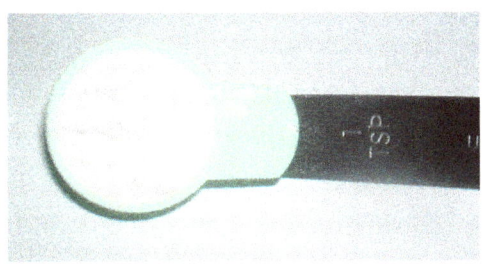
½ Tsp organic, non-aluminium baking powder

1 Tsp pure vanilla extract

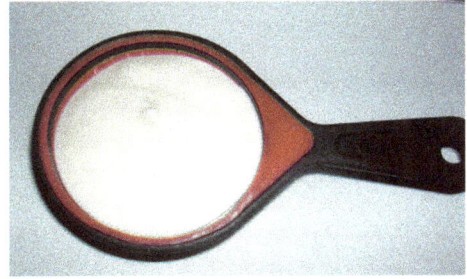
½ cup organic yogurt or milk

Juice of ½ freshly squeezed organic orange and mandarin segments for decoration.

Orange and mandarin-zest cupcakes

Please use either organic milk or yogurt in the following recipe.

Ingredients

80g organic softened salted butter
1/3 cup organic honey
1 large organic egg
1 cup organic self raising flour
½ Tsp organic, non-aluminium baking powder
1 Tsp pure vanilla extract
½ cup organic yogurt or milk
Juice ½ squeezed organic orange
1 organic mandarin

Preparation Time

15 minutes.

Cooking Time

40 minutes or until golden brown.

Oven temperature

Heat oven to 160° before putting the cupcakes into the oven to cook.

Orange zest topping

Butter cream orange topping

60g salted, softened organic butter
1 organic egg yolk
1 dstspn organic honey
1 Tsp pure vanilla extract
2 dstspn organic arrowroot
1-2 dstspn organic milk if required
1 Tsp freshly squeezed organic orange juice.

Cupcake Method

- Beat butter and honey until creamed (if you have an electric beater it's far easier to use than doing this by hand)
- Add egg and beat into butter and honey mixture
- Add the vanilla extract
- Add the juice of the orange
- When the butter, honey, egg, and vanilla are creamed, slowly add the flour, milk, and baking powder
- To keep the mixture light, it is crucial to add the flour slowly
- Beat until the mixture looks a light cream in colour
- Spoon into the cupcake cases and bake.

Orange zest topping

- Beat butter and honey until creamed
- Once the butter and honey are creamed, add the vanilla and egg yolk to the butter mixture
- Slowly add the arrowroot and orange juice
- Cream all ingredients together
- When cool, top your cupcakes with this delicious butter cream and orange icing.
- Add mandarin segment to decorate.

Tip

You can add extra zest to your cupcake mixture by adding a little orange zest of orange peel.

Please ask a parent or adult to help you grate the peel.

Baked cupcakes allowed to cool before icing.

Beaten cupcake mixture in the bleached cupcake cases ready for baking.

Iced cupcakes, ready to eat.

You will need these ingredients to make these mango jelly cupcakes

80g softened organic butter

1/3 cup organic honey

1 organic egg

1 cup organic self raising flour

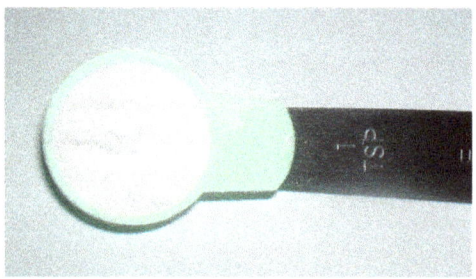

½ Tsp organic, non-aluminium baking powder

1 Tsp pure vanilla extract

½ cup natural organic yogurt or milk

Blitzed mango. To blitz any food ingredient, use a hand food processor with the correct attachment. Please see page 6

Mango jelly cupcakes

Please use either organic milk or yogurt in the following recipe.

Ingredients

80g organic softened salted butter
1/3 cup organic honey
1 large organic egg
1 cup organic self raising flour
½ Tsp organic, non-aluminium baking powder
1 Tsp pure vanilla extract
½ cup organic yogurt or milk
60g pulped organic mango

Preparation Time

15 minutes.

Cooking Time

40 minutes or until golden brown.

Oven temperature

Heat oven to 160° before putting the cupcakes into the oven to cook.

Mango jelly topping

70g blitzed mango flesh
1 dstspn organic gelatin
1 dstspn organic honey
Juice of 1 organic orange
Organic mango cubes for decoration
¼ cup off the boil water to dilute the gelatin.

For more information on gelatin, please see page 16.

Cupcake Method

- Beat butter and honey until creamed (if you have an electric beater it's far easier to use than doing this by hand)
- Add egg and beat into butter and honey mixture
- Add the vanilla extract
- Add the juice of the orange
- When the butter, honey, egg and vanilla are creamed, slowly add the flour, milk and baking powder
- To keep the mixture light, it is crucial to add the flour slowly
- Beat until the mixture looks a light cream in colour
- Spoon into the cupcake cases and bake.

Mango jelly topping

- In a saucepan, slowly warm the mango on the stove
- Add the fresh orange juice and honey to the warming mango
- When sufficiently warm, put gelatin into a small cup and add the off the boil water
- Stir the gelatin and water until almost clear
- Add the gelatin mixture to the warming mango, orange juice and honey
- Keep stirring until all ingredients are well mixed and clear in a golden colour
- Remove from the stove and spoon onto cooled cupcakes, allow to cool until firm
- Add mango cubes as decoration.

Tip

When the mango jelly is almost firm add the mango cubes.

Cupcake mixture in silicone cupcake cases ready for baking.

Cupcakes allowed to cool before adding the mango jelly and mango topping.

Healthy cupcakes that are great for parties, afternoon tea or just any time treats....

You will need these ingredients to make these raspberry jelly cupcakes

80g softened organic butter

1/3 cup organic honey

1 organic egg

1 cup organic self raising flour

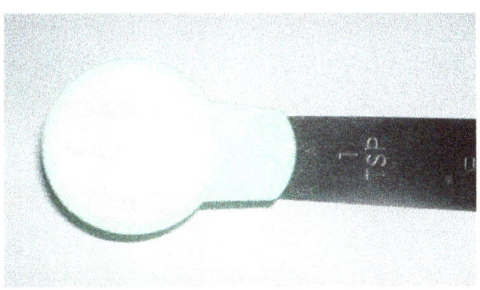

½ Tsp organic, non-aluminium baking powder

1 Tsp pure vanilla extract

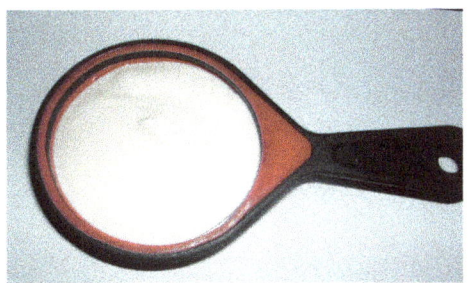

½ cup natural organic yogurt or milk

40g frozen or fresh berries

Raspberry jelly cupcakes

Please use either organic milk or yogurt in the following recipe.

Ingredients

80g organic softened unsalted butter
1/3 cup organic honey
1 cup organic self-raising flour
½ cup organic, yogurt or milk
2 Tspn vanilla extract
1 large organic egg
½ Tsp organic, non-aluminium baking powder
30g organic frozen or fresh raspberries.

Cooking Time

40 minutes or until golden brown.

Oven temperature

Heat oven to 160° before putting the cupcakes in to cook.

Raspberry juice

½ squeezed organic orange
1 Tsp gelatin
1 Tsp organic honey
10g organic frozen or fresh raspberries

Jelly and fruit topping

60g organic frozen or fresh raspberries
1 dstspn organic honey
1 dstspn gelatin
Raspberries to top your cupcakes
½ - 1/3 cup boiled water or warmed fruit juice

Preparation Time 45 minutes.

Method

- Beat butter and honey until creamed (if you have an electric beater it is far easier to use than by hand)
- Add egg and beat into butter and honey mixture
- Add the vanilla extract
- When the butter, honey, egg and vanilla are creamed, slowly add the flour, milk and baking powder
- To keep the mixture light, it is crucial to add the flour slowly
- Beat until the mixture looks a light cream in colour
- Slowly fold in the raspberries
- Spoon into the cupcake cases and bake.
- Allow the cupcakes to completely cool before adding any toppings.

Raspberry juice

- Squeeze the orange half
- Add the honey and raspberries to the juice
- Mix the gelatin into the orange, raspberry, and honey mixture and warm in the microwave
- Lightly brush the cupcake top before adding crushed raspberry jelly to the top of the cakes
- Top with fresh raspberries or fruit of your choice.

Jelly fruit topping

- Allow the raspberries to thaw if using frozen
- Warm the honey and stir through the fruit
- Add a hot water or fruit juice to the gelatin, and mix well
- Mix the gelatin into the raspberry and honey mixture and allow to set
- Once set, mash the topping with a vegetable masher
- Spoon onto cupcake tops.

Tips

Allow the cupcakes to be completely cold before adding the jelly topping.

Cupcake raspberry mixture in silicone cupcake cases ready for baking.

Cupcakes just out of the oven.

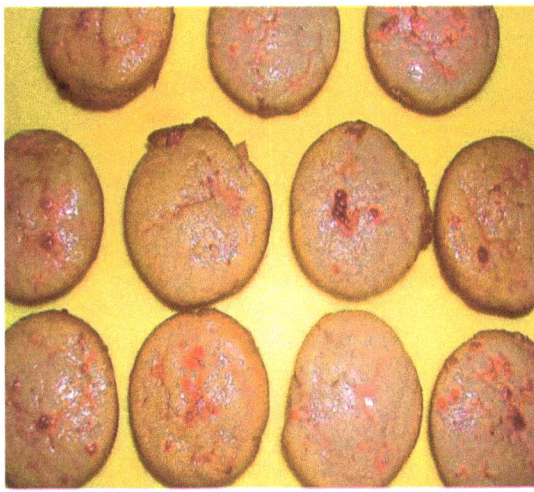

Once cooled, lightly brush and coat cupcakes with the raspberry juice mixture.

Jelly topping: If possible, allow the jelly to set overnight.

The firm jelly is mashed with a vegetable masher this gives the appearance of jelly crystals.

The cupcakes are coated with the raspberry juice prior to adding the jelly topping.

You will need these ingredients to make these chocolate cupcakes

80g softened organic butter

1/3 cup organic honey

1 organic egg

1 cup organic self raising flour

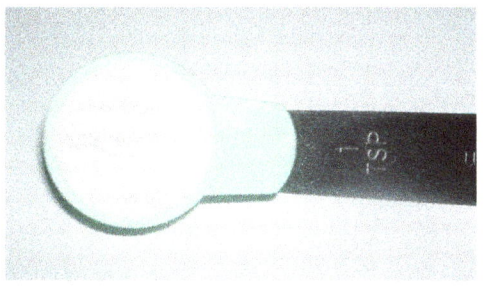
½ Tsp organic, non-aluminium baking powder

1 Tsp pure vanilla extract

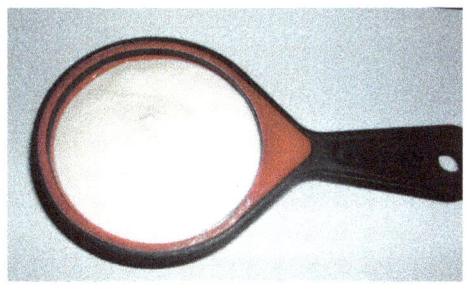
½ cup natural organic yogurt or milk

2 dstpn organic dark, drinking powdered chocolate or organic cocoa

Chocolate cupcakes

Please use either organic milk or yogurt in the following recipe.

Ingredients

80g organic softened salted butter
1/3 cup organic honey
1 large organic egg
1 cup organic self raising flour
½ Tsp organic, non-aluminium baking powder
1 Tsp pure vanilla extract
½ cup organic natural yogurt or milk
2 dstspn organic dark, drinking powdered chocolate or organic cocoa.

Cooking Time

40 minutes or until golden brown.

Oven temperature

Heat oven to 160° before putting the cupcakes in to cook.

Butter chocolate cream topping

60g organic butter
1 organic egg yolk
1 dstspn organic honey
1 Tsp pure vanilla extract
2 dstspn organic arrowroot
1 dstspn organic dark, drinking powdered chocolate or organic cocoa
1-2 dstspn organic milk if required.

Preparation Time

45 minutes.

Method

- Beat butter, egg, and honey until creamed (if an electric beater is available, it is far easier to use than doing this by hand)
- Add the vanilla extract and yogurt
- When the butter, honey, egg. and vanilla are creamed, slowly add the flour, powdered chocolate, and baking powder.

(To keep the mixture light, it is crucial to add the flour and chocolate powder slowly.)

- Beat until the mixture looks a light cream in colour
- Spoon into the cupcake cases and bake. Makes 12 cupcakes.

Butter chocolate cream topping

- Beat butter and honey until creamed (if you have an electric beater, it will make a smooth paste)
- Once the butter and honey are creamed, add the vanilla and egg yolk to the butter mixture
- Slowly add the arrowroot and chocolate powder
- Cream all ingredients together
- Spoon a small amount onto each cupcake
- With the back of a fork, swirl to form a rosette shape.

Tip

Like all cakes, cupcakes are better served fresh on the day they are baked. However, cupcakes can be made earlier and frozen. When defrosted, blitz in the microwave for 2 or 3 seconds, then add the toppings.

You can use different fruit for topping cupcakes

Just cooked chocolate cupcakes

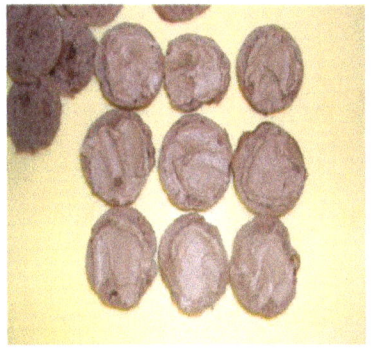

The tops of the cupcakes are removed ready for adding the chocolate cream

The tops are re-attached with chocolate icing topping

Fruit topping of your choice. Here, I have used golden kiwi fruit and fresh berries.

Honey and sugar-free blueberry cupcakes

Juvenile onset diabetes or Diabetes Type 1 has increased over the years. More children are required to work with and manage this health condition. As a mother of a diabetic child, I can speak from my experience and know that some young diabetics miss out at birthday parties and on special occasions. While all forms of carbohydrate needs to be understood by the diabetic and the family, there are ways of giving these beautiful children a little treat every now and again. Remembering that even complex carbohydrate, through the body's system, converts to glucose.

Glucose is energy building and extracted by the human body from the natural foods we eat including fruit and vegetables. Natural glucose helps the brain to function and the body to be energised. Extracted sugar from cane or beet are empty calories that only contribute to ill health and weight gain and interfere with our hormone balance; this interference contributes to many obesity problems seen in the world communities today.

You will need these ingredients to make these honey and sugar-free blueberry cupcakes

80g softened organic butter

1/3 cup organic honey

1 organic egg

1 cup organic self raising flour

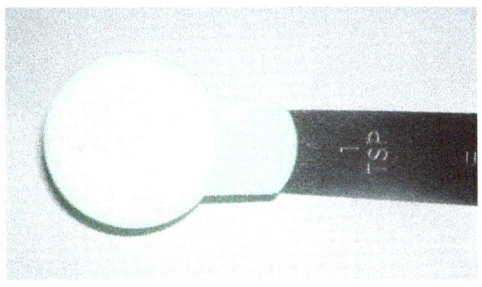

½ Tsp organic, non-aluminium baking powder

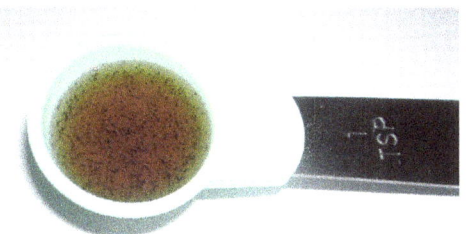

1 Tsp pure vanilla extract

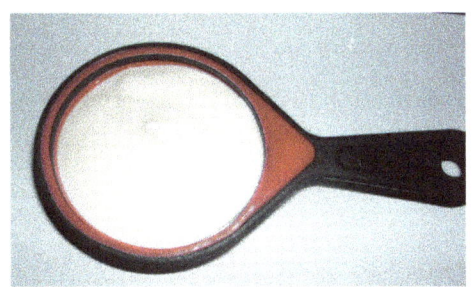

½ cup natural organic yogurt or milk

Mashed berries

Honey and sugar-free blueberry cupcakes

Ingredients

80g organic softened salted butter
1 cup organic self raising flour
1/3 cup organic, milk
2 Tsp vanilla extract
1 large organic egg
¾ Tsp organic, non-aluminium baking powder
6 scoops Pure Stevia

Cooking Time

40 minutes or until golden brown.

Oven temperature

Heat oven to 160° before putting the cupcakes in to cook.

Preparation Time

45 minutes.

Tips

Allow the cupcakes to be completely cold before adding the jelly insert.

Method

- Beat butter and Stevia and egg until creamed (if you have an electric beater it is far easier to use than by hand)
- Add the vanilla extract
- When the butter, Stevia, egg and vanilla are creamed, slowly add the flour, milk and baking powder
- To keep the mixture light, it is crucial to add the flour slowly
- Beat until the mixture looks a light cream in colour
- Spoon into the cupcake cases and bake.

Cupcakes straight from the oven. Because of the lack of sugar or honey, these cakes do not brown on the top like other cakes, they do however, brown on the underside.

Sugar-free blueberry jelly filling for cupcakes and other cake fillings

Ingredients

250g frozen or fresh organic blueberries or berries of your choice
½ squeezed organic orange
3 scoops Pure Stevia
2½ dstspn pure gelatin
1/3 cup boiled water
Organic cream or natural organic yogurt for topping

Preparation Time

45 minutes.

Setting time

3 hours or overnight. Allow the cupcakes to be completely cold before cutting into two and adding the jelly filling.

Jelly fruit filling

- Allow the blueberries to thaw if using frozen
- Add the boiled water to the gelatin and mix well
- Add the Stevia
- Add the fruit, while stirring into the mixture
- Line a container, depending on the number of cupcakes you make, with BPA-free cling film
- Allow the depth of your jelly to be about 1½ cm (1½ ml)
- Once made, leave in the fridge to set
- Cut cooled cupcakes into halves
- Cut circles of blueberry jelly, add to bottom half of cake, then top with top half of cake
- Garnish with organic cream or yogurt and add a fresh berry for garnish.

You can use a shape for cutting out your jelly shape; I have used the round shape to fit the shape of the cupcake.

Your choice of organic fruit can be used.

To add more fun, use different shapes for cutting the jelly.

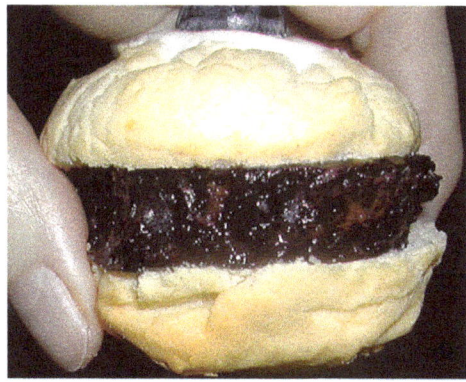

Compared to the original cupcake, these are lighter and drier in texture. They are a delightful change enjoyed by children and adults alike.

Little treats for special people...

In my school life, I am still teaching children with diabetes, I know their journey and like many life-long health conditions, Type One Diabetes does not take a holiday or break.

These cupcakes are topped with organic, natural yogurt and fresh organic blueberries.

Sugar is used in many bought cakes. Sugar acts like scaffolding in cooking. This, is why, many bought cupcakes and muffins have that sweet, gooey consistency. Sugar also allows the mixture to rise while baking. The sweetness of sugar works on the brain's receptors and once eaten requires more of the poison that we all call sugar. Sugar is an opiate and the more you eat, the more you will develop the craving for sugar.

You will need these ingredients to make these cheese and honey cupcakes

80g softened organic butter

1/3 cup organic honey

1 organic egg

1 cup organic self raising flour

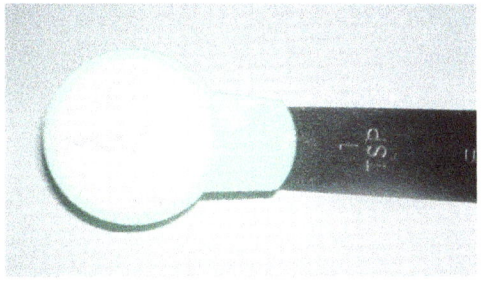

½ Tsp organic, non-aluminium baking powder

1 Tsp pure vanilla extract

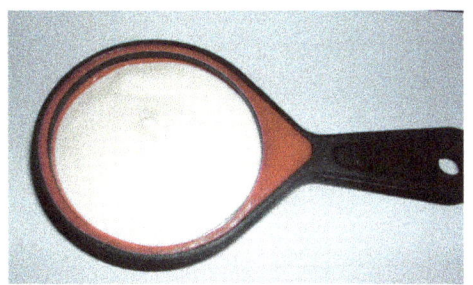

½ cup natural organic yogurt or milk

2 dstspn grated Grana Padano

Cheese and honey cupcakes

Please use either organic milk or yogurt in the following recipe.

Ingredients

80g organic softened salted butter
1/3 cup organic honey
1 large organic egg
1 cup organic self raising flour
½ Tsp organic, non-aluminium baking powder
1 Tsp pure vanilla extract
½ cup organic natural yogurt or milk
2 dstspn grated Grana Padano cheese

Cooking Time

40 minutes or until golden brown.

Oven temperature

Heat oven to 160° before putting the cupcakes in to cook.

Topping

Sprinkle with Grana Padano cheese

Preparation Time

45 minutes.

Tip

Grana Padano cheese is a completely natural hard cheese. It is made from whole milk where cows are allowed to naturally graze on clean pastures where they live a happy, and stress-free life.

Method

- Beat butter, egg, and honey until creamed (if an electric beater is available, it is far easier to use than doing this by hand)
- Add the vanilla extract and yogurt
- When the butter, honey, egg. and vanilla are creamed, slowly add the flour, powdered chocolate, and baking powder.

(To keep the mixture light, it is crucial to add the flour and cheese slowly.)

- Beat until the mixture looks a light cream in colour
- Spoon into the cupcake cases and bake. Makes 12 cupcakes.

Tip

Like all cakes, cupcakes are better served fresh on the day they are baked. However, cupcakes can be made earlier and frozen. When defrosted, blitz in the microwave for 2 or 3 seconds, serve with a delicious range of toppings.

The inside of the silicone cupcake case is coated with organic olive oil.

The cupcake mixture is in the cupcake cases ready for baking.

Cheese and honey cupcakes are delicious with olives, pieces of cut cheese and make a great afternoon tea.

Cheese and a cheesy cupcake make a treat for after school.

Add berries, carrot sticks and cubes of cheese for a school lunch.

All of the recipes in this book are made from organic foods and contain no nasty food molecules. Children are receptive and want to know the difference between healthy and unhealthy food.

Good Food Molecule   Nasty Food Molecule

www.how2books.com.au

booksforreadingonline.com

www.ingramcontent.com/pod-product-compliance
Lightning Source LLC
Chambersburg PA
CBHW061536010526
44107CB00066B/2889